The Power of Praye

# *Impartations*

# *From*

# *Heaven*

## A 12- day Morning Prayer Devotional

### Ursula McClary

Ursula McClary © Copyrights 2022 The Power of Prayer and Devotion *Impartations From Heaven* A 12- day Morning Prayer Devotional ISBN: 978-1-947437-29-6

Divine Favors Books Publications
Divinepublisher2022@outlook.com

## Table of Contents
**Pages**

This book is dedicated to You Lord Jesus!

This devotional would not exist, had it not been for Your steadfast, faithful, and guiding Spirit. There are no words that can describe how grateful I am to You, precious Lover of my soul. I am very aware that the reason I am here is because of Your undeserved love and favor, protection, provision, mercy, and grace. Why do You love me like You do? I am still in awe of the miracle of new heart You have given me. You have a way to keep in awestruck wonder of who You are. I will continue to strive to give You my best as You change me more and more. You have shown me so much of what You want to do through me. Too often my own fears and doubts reduced my speed of walking with you and threatened to abort the vision. Your unfailing love always finds me, and You will not let me give up. It is amazing to me that You would use me, knowing all about me. You have taught me and still teach me what unconditional love is and this gift compels me to love others. Your ways are so much higher than mine and Your thoughts higher than mine. I will forever worship You and trust You with my life, because You will never disappoint me. I am thrilled over our continuous journey together.

To You, my God, be glory forever and ever. Amen.

Forever in You,

Ursula

## Acknowledgements

With special thanks: Thank you to all who have undergirded me in prayer throughout this project.

To my husband Van McClary: Thank you for your support, your love and wise counsel. I love you and thank God for you.

To Sharveace, Orlando, sweet Omari, and Alesha: Thank you for your love and for living. Your very existence gives me so much joy and strength. I love you.

To Abbey and Amos: Thank you for the outpouring of your love, prayers, and support. Thank you for always giving me the extra push. Your life and walk with the Lord inspire me daily. I love you

To my God-children Wil- Gregory, Jonathan and L.J: You are gifts from the Lord, and I am forever grateful for the love you add to my life. I love you.

To Dr. Linda Chinn: I am forever grateful for you. Thank you for your love, support, prayers, your wise counsel, your honesty, and your graciousness to be there for me even when your schedule is full.

To Tammy: Thank you for your endless love and encouragement.

To Nikole, my sister and warrior partner: Thank you for being real with me. Your prayers and love have made all the difference. I love you.

To Mia, my sister from the heart: I love you so much and always feel your prayers. Thank you for YOU!!!

To my sweet Gail: Thank you for your love, encouragement, and meticulous help on this project. I love you.

To my Pastor Bishop Dale C. Bronner and First Lady Dr. Nina Bronner: Thank you for your covering, your love and the richness in your teaching. I am richer in my Spirit because of you. I have learned so much and am eternally grateful.

To Mary: Thank you for your love and professionalism during this project.

# Foreword

Impartations From Heaven is sure to whet, stir up and increase your appetite for more of God's Word. I assure you, that when you're through reading this devotional, you're going to long for more. You're going to yearn to hear God speak directly to you as He does Ursula!

We met when we were both Sunday school teachers at a mega church and I've known Ursula for over 20 years. There is no doubt in my mind that this book came out of her life of worship. My first encounter with her was where I saw humility personified in a leader. I met someone who genuinely, unequivocally, and unashamedly loves God, His Word, and His people. I've been places where when she walked into the room, the atmosphere changed, love was palpable, grace and mercy were available, and you just KNEW everything was going to be OK.

She's one of those people by whom I'm constantly fascinated because she connects everything to God, and I do mean everything! And because of that, you will find your breakthrough in the power of the simplicity in which Impartations From Heaven was written.

As Ursula shares how God spoke to her in real life events, you will know beyond a shadow of a doubt that God does speak to people! It is not just an Old Testament 'thing'.

Enjoy it! Another book is coming!!!

Dr. Linda P. Chinn

## Introduction

In these past couple of years, we have seen and gone through pandemics, racial injustice, school shootings, governmental issues, floods, fires and earthquakes. I truly believe that the "shaking" of our world and what we have experienced individually has all happened with purpose. These things can be used by God, or they are sent by God. We cannot necessarily determine the reason of these things happening, but some can be traced back to rebellion against God.

The Lord knows the plans He has for us (see Jeremiah 29:11), but our rebellion against Him causes us to experience life in ways He never planned for us. Rebellion against God's authority was humanity's first sin (see Genesis 3) and continues to be our downfall. Many of our lives are filled with sin and rebellion, as well as many things that are unproductive and fruitless. This choice of lifestyle leaves no room for God's plan and His purpose to flourish in and through us.

A "busy" life does not necessarily mean that what we are doing is our God-ordained purpose. It may leave us in seemingly "happy" places, but in the long run we will be confronted with the harassing question, "What is the meaning of my life?"

God created us for Him (see Colossians 1:16). Every human was birthed into this world *on, with* and *for* a great purpose. God created us in His image in order to glorify Him through our lives. He has a divine plan and purpose for us. Unfortunately, we were born into sin and therefore blind. Until we are born again, we will not be able to see Gods great plan-His kingdom (see John 3:3).

Aimless or God-void lives are empty lives. Empty lives do not impact others and can leave us depressed, frustrated and bitter.

God's sovereignty and love, permits trials and affliction. The "shaking" He allows will remove unfruitful things from our lives and will lead us to whom and to what really matters- our relationship with our Creator and Lord (See Hebrews 12: 25-29)!

*It is the shaking and darkness that precedes the Greater Glory!*

The revelation of who we are and why we are here comes from an intimate relationship with our Savior and Lord Jesus Christ. As we surrender and lay down our worries and anxieties, we enter into the rest of God.

It is in His presence, in our communion with Him, where we receive guidance and direction.

It was through prayer, meditation and the guidance of the Holy Spirit this devotional was birthed.

In general, a devotional can be a great tool to lead us into the presence of God. However, a devotional should never substitute our study time with the Lord. The Bible declares in 2 Timothy 2:15 (Amplified version) "Study and do your best to present yourself to God approved, a workman [tested by trial] who has no reason to be ashamed, accurately handling and skillfully teaching the word of truth".

I encourage you to expose yourself fully to the Word of God and ask Holy Spirit to reveal truth. He is our teacher (see John 16:13, John 14:26). He has been sent to live in and through you, to think through you, to teach and to instruct you.

It is important to understand the word of God in its fullness and Holy Spirit will guide you into all truth.

Biblical content, context and culture are not necessarily found in devotionals alone.

This devotional is written to inspire you and prayerfully stimulate a more thorough Bible study. I encourage you to compare scripture with scripture, consult different Bible study resources and study aids such as a Lexicon and Bible concordance. Always involve your Teacher, the Lover of Your Soul in reading and studying the word of God.

My prayers are with you as you read and work through this devotional.

May you be the recipient of revelation and new impartations from heaven

May the Lord open your eyes that you may see wondrous truth in His word

May He reveal Himself to you in even greater ways

# Stay Filled

Devotional:

There's no doubt that the Lord wants us to be filled with His word and with His Spirit. (Ephesians 5:18). He knows that the word of God is our weapon against sin. If we don't fill ourselves with the word of God, we will be filled with something else. We see a good example of this in the life of Ananias and Sapphira (see Acts 5). Their hypocritical behavior proved that they allowed space for the enemy of their soul. On the contrary, the apostle Peter was filled with the power of the Spirit and was able to discern Ananias lie.

The devil is looking for people who are not filled with God's word and His Spirit. He deceives them to walk after the desires of their flesh, which ultimately is a doorway for Satan to enter in and take possession of their life.

God provided a way of escape through His son Jesus Christ. As we accept God's gift of love and abide in His word, we will no longer be slaves to sin. He is faithful to cover and protect us. He gives us power to walk in the Spirit, so we will not fulfill the desires of our flesh. Choose Him daily, fill yourself with the word of God and stay close to His heart. (See John 15)

Scripture: Acts 4:31

And when they had prayed, the place where they were meeting together was shaken [a sign of God's presence]; and they were all filled with the Holy Spirit and began to speak the word of God with boldness and courage.

Prayer:

Thank you so much, Father, for Your abundance of grace and mercy in my life. Thank You for life and peace in Your word. There is so much comfort and joy in Your presence. Please continue to draw me with loving kindness. Thank You for keeping me in your tender care.

In Jesus' Name I pray

Amen

Scripture Reference:

Acts 13:9

But Saul, who was also called Paul, filled with the Holy Spirit, looked intently at him.

Ephesians 5:18

And do not get drunk with wine, for that is debauchery, but be filled with the Spirit.

Acts 6:3

Therefore, brothers, pick out from among you seven men of good repute, full of the Spirit and of wisdom, whom we will appoint to this duty.

Luke 1:67

And his father Zechariah was filled with the Holy Spirit and prophesied, saying.

Romans 15:13

May the God of hope fill you with all joy and peace in believing, so that by the power of the Holy Spirit you may abound in hope.

Psalm 71:8

My mouth is filled with your praise, declaring your splendor all day long.


Matthew 5:6

Blessed are those who hunger and thirst for righteousness, for they will be filled.

Colossians 2:9, 10

For in Christ all the fullness of the Deity lives in bodily form, and in Christ you have been brought to fullness. He is the head over every power and authority.

Psalm 36:8

They are filled with food from your house, and you allow them to drink from the river of your delicacies

Personal Reflections:

---

# Pray and Obey

Devotional:

Prayer and obedience are a lifestyle for the believer. As a matter of fact, obedience is the highest form of worship. As we know from scripture, Lucifer (who is Satan, who is also called the devil) was thrown down from heaven, the place of worship (Ezekiel 28:14; Isaiah 14:12-15; Revelations 12:9). He lost his place of worship. Now his main objective is to keep us separated from God.

He uses distractions to keep us out of the presence of God. The enemy of our soul wants us to hear every other voice, except the voice of the Shepherd. He wants us to stay in sin. Satan's plan is to mess up our hearing, so we won't follow God's voice. It is God's voice that leads us into God's will.

God's love is so much greater than any of our sins or shortcomings. When we have tasted God's goodness, we will not be able to be apart from God for a long time. We eventually will sense the hand of God on our lives. His loving Spirit will convict us, so that we confess our sin and turn our hearts to God. It is not until we connect with Him again, acknowledge our sins and allow Him to lead the way, which will allow us to walk in His peace again. Make prayer and obedience your lifestyle.

Scripture:

Psalm 32: 1-11

Blessed is the one whose transgressions are forgiven, whose sins are covered. Blessed is the one whose sin the Lord does not count against them and in whose spirit is no deceit. When I kept silent, my bones wasted away through my groaning all day long. For day and night your hand was heavy on me; my strength was sapped as in the heat of summer. Then I acknowledged my sin to you and did not cover up my iniquity. I said, "I will confess my transgressions to the Lord." And you forgave the guilt of my sin. Therefore, let all the faithful pray to you while you may be found; surely the rising of the mighty waters will not reach them. You are my hiding place; you will protect me from trouble and surround me with songs of deliverance. I will instruct you and teach you in the way you should go; I will counsel you with my loving eye on you.

Do not be like the horse or the mule, which have no understanding but must be controlled by bit and bridle or they will not come to you.

Many are the woes of the wicked, but the Lord's unfailing love surrounds the one who trusts in him. Rejoice in the Lord and be glad, you are righteous; sing, all you who are upright in heart!


Prayer:

Father, Thank You for Your faithfulness! Your mercies are new every morning and Your compassion towards me never fails. Thank You for drawing me back to You when I am distracted or sin against You. Help me to daily take Your hand and walk with You, knowing You will lead me. I will trust Your perfect plan to follow and obey Your instructions. I will not lean to my own understanding but acknowledge you in all my ways. I praise and I love You Father!!!

In Jesus' Name I pray

Amen

Scripture Reference:

John 15:9

"As the Father has loved me, so have I loved you. Now remain in my love.

2 Corinthians 10:5

We demolish arguments and every pretension that sets itself up against the knowledge of God, and we take captive every thought to make it obedient to Christ.

Revelations 14:12

This calls for patient endurance on the part of the people of God who keep his commands and remain faithful to Jesus.

John 15:14

You are my friends if you do what I command.

2 John 1:6

And this is love: that we walk in obedience to his commands. As you have heard from the beginning, his command is that you walk in love.

Luke 11:28

He replied, "Blessed rather are those who hear the word of God and obey it."

Romans 5:19

For just as through the disobedience of the one man the many were made sinners, so also through the obedience of the one man the many will be made righteous.

1 Peter 1:14

As obedient children do not conform to the evil desires you had when you lived in ignorance.

Find new times in the day or night to devote to the Lord and commit to them. God loves our time with Him. Obedience is the highest form of worship. Allow Holy Spirit to reveal any areas of disobedience:

------------------------------------------------------------------------

------------------------------------------------------------------------

------------------------------------------------------------------------

------------------------------------------------------------------------

------------------------------------------------------------------------

------------------------------------------------------------------------

------------------------------------------------------------------------

------------------------------------------------------------------------

------------------------------------------------------------------------

------------------------------------------------------------------------

------------------------------------------------------------------------

------------------------------------------------------------------------

------------------------------------------------------------------------

------------------------------------------------------------------------

------------------------------------------------------------------------

------------------------------------------------------------------------

------------------------------------------------------------------------

------------------------------------------------------------------------

------------------------------------------------------------------------

------------------------------------------------------------------------

# Shine your light

Devotion:

Letting our light shine is a decision. Even though certain experiences in life could present a challenge to letting our light shine, nevertheless we are left with a choice. My mom was diagnosed with cancer a few years ago. It was during the same time that a doctor's visit revealed blood clots in my husband's body. The doctor made it very clear that his life was at high risk. I had to make up my mind to speak life and trust God's word during this very trying time. My mom eventually lost her battle to cancer but gained eternal life. My husband went through several surgeries and survived. Glory to God!!!!

It was not easy, but the Lord was gracious to carry us through one of the hardest seasons in our life. He walked alongside us and graced us to shine His light through it all.

Today I was reminded again of the power of shining our light. I had to return to an auto shop after a repair service, because my car still did not sound right. The sweet and professional lady at the front desk caught my attention with her graceful and joyful spirit. After the mechanics completed the service, I had a chance to talk with her again. In our conversation she shared that she had just lost her daughter as well as another close family member. She said she was getting a little weak. Immediately we embraced and we prayed together.

In spite of the grief, she felt inside, she made a conscious decision to let her light shine. Nobody knew what she was going through, because of the beautiful light in her. She chose to let God shine through her. He met her with renewed strength and grace.

Relationship with Jesus Christ enables us to choose light over darkness.

Scripture:

Matthew 5:16 KJV

Let your light so shine before men, that they may see your good works, and glorify your Father which is in heaven.


Prayer:

Father, shine through me even when darkness surrounds me. Your life in me empowers me to shine. Remind me to shine Your light especially in the valleys, for You are with me.

In Jesus' Name I pray

Amen

Scripture Reference:

Matthew 5:14-16

"You are the light of the world. A city set on a hill cannot be hidden. Nor do people light a lamp and put it under a basket, but on a stand, and it gives light to all in the house. In the same way, let your light shine before others, so that they may see your good works and give glory to your Father who is in heaven.

John 8:12

Again, Jesus spoke to them, saying, "I am the light of the world. Whoever follows me will not walk in darkness but will have the light of life."

Ephesians 5:8

For ye were sometimes darkness, but now are ye light in the Lord: walk as children of light:

1 Corinthians 10:31

Whether therefore ye eat, or drink, or whatsoever ye do, do all to the glory of God.

Luke 8:16

No man, when he hath lighted a candle, covereth it with a vessel, or putteth it under a bed; but setteth it on a candlestick, that they which enter in may see the light.

Romans 13:11, 12

Do this, knowing the time that it is already the hour for you to awaken from sleep; for now, salvation is nearer to us than when we believed. The night is almost gone, and the day is near. Therefore, let us lay aside the deeds of darkness and put on the armor of light.

Journal and celebrate the times where God used you to shine your light.
Acknowledge areas where God wants access to shine through you:

---------------------------------------------------------------

---------------------------------------------------------------

---------------------------------------------------------------

---------------------------------------------------------------

---------------------------------------------------------------

---------------------------------------------------------------

---------------------------------------------------------------

---------------------------------------------------------------

---------------------------------------------------------------

---------------------------------------------------------------

---------------------------------------------------------------

---------------------------------------------------------------

---------------------------------------------------------------

---------------------------------------------------------------

---------------------------------------------------------------

---------------------------------------------------------------

---------------------------------------------------------------

---------------------------------------------------------------

---------------------------------------------------------------

---------------------------------------------------------------

---------------------------------------------------------------

---------------------------------------------------------------

---------------------------------------------------------------

# In Christ

Devotion:

Everything we need in this life is found in Him. It is IN Christ that we live, move and have our being. To believe in Christ is to be crucified with Him and to have Him replace your sinful nature with a new nature. We now live by faith in the Son of God. Moreover, Jesus gave Himself for our sin because He loved us so much (see Galatians 2:19, 20). The moment we lose sight of that, we will begin to struggle to move by the Spirit and we tend to yield to the dictates of the flesh.

When we fully understand that our flesh cannot and does not want to please God, we can graciously accept the new life God gave us in Christ. Think of it this way: Your old nature is buried IN Him. Let your old nature "Rest in Peace".

Learn to do things God's way, by simply obeying His word. The "New "can be scary at first, but embracing it brings a tremendous amount of freedom and deep joy.

God is encouraging us not to fear, because He will help us and undergird us to walk out His will.

Scripture:

Romans 8:1

There is therefore now no condemnation for those who are IN Christ Jesus.

Prayer:

Thank You Father for the new life You gave me.  You empower me by Your Spirit to choose Your way. I am so grateful, that even when I fail at times Your precious blood covers me. Thank You for Your patience with me and Your lovingkindness towards me. Your love is incredible!!! Please help me to love You more by simply choosing You.

In Jesus' Name I pray

Amen

Scripture Reference:

2 Corinthians 5:17

Therefore, if anyone is in Christ, he is a new creature; the old things passed away; behold, new things have come.

Galatians 6:15

In Christ Jesus neither circumcision availeth anything, nor uncircumcision, but a new creature.

Ephesians 4:24

…and put on the new self, which in the likeness of God has been created in righteousness and holiness of the truth.

Colossians 3:10

…and have put on the new self who is being renewed to a true knowledge according to the image of the One who created him—

Romans 6:4

Therefore, we have been buried with Him through baptism into death, so that as Christ was raised from the dead through the glory of the Father, so we too might walk in newness of life.

1 Peter 1:3

Praise be to the God and Father of our Lord Jesus Christ! In his great mercy he has given us new birth into a living hope through the resurrection of Jesus Christ from the dead.

Is there an area in which the Lord is convicting you? Pray and journal these areas; surrender them in prayer:

-------------------------------------------------------------------

-------------------------------------------------------------------

-------------------------------------------------------------------

-------------------------------------------------------------------

-------------------------------------------------------------------

-------------------------------------------------------------------

-------------------------------------------------------------------

-------------------------------------------------------------------

-------------------------------------------------------------------

-------------------------------------------------------------------

-------------------------------------------------------------------

-------------------------------------------------------------------

-------------------------------------------------------------------

-------------------------------------------------------------------

-------------------------------------------------------------------

-------------------------------------------------------------------

-------------------------------------------------------------------

-------------------------------------------------------------------

-------------------------------------------------------------------

-------------------------------------------------------------------

-------------------------------------------------------------------

-------------------------------------------------------------------

-------------------------------------------------------------------

# Rest in Him

Devotional:

Rest is a crucial part of our physical and spiritual well-being. We may feel that we always must be doing something for the Lord. Sometimes doing is simply "being" - resting and knowing who we are in Christ and walking out who we are. An orange or apple does not come forth on its own; but it grows from a tree. An apple tree usually produces fruit from late summer through fall. Even though apples do not grow on the tree during the winter and spring seasons, that does not stop it from being an apple tree. The fruit comes in the right season. The fruit is the "by-product" of what it is.

Likewise, with a child of God, the fruit, gifts and work are by-products of who we are. So, on those days or seasons when there is "nothing" on the agenda, just rest in Him until the next assignment.

You will surely bear fruit in the right season as you continue to abide in Him.

Scripture:

Acts 17:28

For in him we live and move and have our being.' As some of your own poets have said, 'We are his offspring.'

Prayer:

Thank You so much Father, for sweet rest in You. Me in You, and You in me. Thank You that You are not a harsh taskmaster, but a loving Father who is always more concerned about my relationship with You, then what I "do" for You. As I seek Your kingdom and righteousness first, all these other things will be added to me. I praise and honor You!!Thank You for loving me with such an incredible and unconditional love!!

In Jesus' Name I pray

Amen

Scripture Reference:

2 Corinthians 5:17

Therefore, if anyone is in Christ, he is a new creation. The old has passed away; behold, the new has come.

Psalm 55:6

I said, "Oh, that I had the wings of a dove! I would fly away and be at rest.

Jeremiah 31:26

At this I awoke and looked, and my sleep was pleasant to me

Isaiah 30:15

For thus said the Lord God, the Holy One of Israel, "In returning and rest you shall be saved; in quietness and in trust shall be your strength." But you were unwilling,

Psalm 62:1

Truly my soul finds rest in God; my salvation comes from him.

Matthew 8:24

And behold, there arose a great storm on the sea, so that the boat was being swamped by the waves; but he was asleep.

Are you constantly "doing something"? What is the root of your busyness? Are you seeking approval through your works? Are you a people- pleaser or a God-pleaser? Ask Holy Spirit to guide you in your reflection and response:

---------------------------------------------------------------
---------------------------------------------------------------
---------------------------------------------------------------
---------------------------------------------------------------
---------------------------------------------------------------
---------------------------------------------------------------
---------------------------------------------------------------
---------------------------------------------------------------
---------------------------------------------------------------
---------------------------------------------------------------
---------------------------------------------------------------
---------------------------------------------------------------
---------------------------------------------------------------
---------------------------------------------------------------
---------------------------------------------------------------
---------------------------------------------------------------
---------------------------------------------------------------
---------------------------------------------------------------
---------------------------------------------------------------
---------------------------------------------------------------
---------------------------------------------------------------
---------------------------------------------------------------

# Your High place

Devotional:

God is always calling us to see from His perspective. Through Jesus Christ we were brought near to Him. We were seated with Him in heavenly places (read Ephesians 2:6).

God knows that we will experience test, trials and temptations. Keeping a kingdom perspective during these times, help us to persevere and overcome. As we set our mind to "Get up", we are already a step ahead. This is easier said than done at times. We must realize that the battle is in the mind. As we make the choice to take small steps, we eventually will "climb" the mountains of life with His help, we ultimately find ourselves on top of the mountain. We now see from God's perspective. We are gifted with a testimony how we overcame and end up proclaiming God's faithfulness.

Scripture:

Isaiah 40:9 NKJV

O Zion, You who bring good tidings, *Get up* into the high mountain; O Jerusalem, You who bring good tidings, Lift up your voice with strength, Lift it up, be not afraid; Say to the cities of Judah, "Behold your God!"

Prayer:

Father, help me to stay encouraged when I find myself in valley places. Help me to remember that You are building a testimony in me to encourage others. You have already made me an overcomer. Thank You for always helping me to climb the mountains of life victoriously.

In Jesus' Name I pray

Amen

Scripture Reference:

Isaiah 35:2

It will bloom profusely and rejoice with joy and singing. The glory of Lebanon will be given to it, the splendor of Carmel and Sharon. They will see the glory of the LORD, the splendor of our God.

Habakkuk 3:19

The Lord God is my strength, and He has made my feet like hinds' feet, and makes me walk on my high places.

Deuteronomy 32:13

"He made him ride on the high places of the earth, and he ate the produce of the field; and He made him suck honey from the rock and oil from the flinty rock

Psalm 18:33

He makes my feet like hinds' feet, and sets me upon my high places

Psalm 18:33 AMPC

He makes my feet like hinds' feet [able to stand firmly or make progress on the dangerous heights of testing and trouble]; He sets me securely upon my high places.

Psalm 18:29

For in You I can charge an army, and with my God I can scale a wall.

Psalm 18:36

You broaden the path beneath me so that my ankles do not give way.

Is there a particular area in your life, where you need to change your perspective?
Write what the Lord reveals to you:

-------------------------------------------------------------------------

-------------------------------------------------------------------------

-------------------------------------------------------------------------

-------------------------------------------------------------------------

-------------------------------------------------------------------------

-------------------------------------------------------------------------

-------------------------------------------------------------------------

-------------------------------------------------------------------------

-------------------------------------------------------------------------

-------------------------------------------------------------------------

-------------------------------------------------------------------------

-------------------------------------------------------------------------

-------------------------------------------------------------------------

-------------------------------------------------------------------------

-------------------------------------------------------------------------

-------------------------------------------------------------------------

-------------------------------------------------------------------------

-------------------------------------------------------------------------

-------------------------------------------------------------------------

-------------------------------------------------------------------------

-------------------------------------------------------------------------

-------------------------------------------------------------------------

# GROWTH

Devotional:

There is no doubt, that God wants us to continue to grow and develop.

When my daughter was younger, she often complained of pain in her knees and arms. The doctor informed us that she simply had "growing pains".

Growth and development are often laced with pain. In order to grow in patience, we have to endure the pain of *waiting* for a promise to come to pass. In order to grow in love, the most cantankerous people are showing up in our lives. In order to grow in knowledge, we must undergo the discipline of study. Growing pains!!!

As a child of God, we are called to walk by faith. It is impossible to please God without it.

It is vital to walk by faith especially during challenging times. Walking by faith, means we BELIEVE and TRUST God's promise is coming to pass. In other words, we have no doubt-we know that all things will work together for our good, while the situation has not changed yet.

It takes effort and intentionality to walk by faith. Our emotions, feelings or situations DO NOT determine if we have faith or not. It is, and remains, our trust in His word that determines whether we have faith or not. I can still have faith, even if my feelings don't line up. It is the enemy's lies that make us think differently. I can walk in the Spirit, while my soul (will, mind and emotions) may not have lined up yet. It is your choice of walking in the Spirit that will cause your soul (will, mind and emotions) to follow.

Choosing to pray, praise and trust especially in challenging seasons causes growth and development.

Scripture:

2 Peter 1:5-10 NLT

In view of all this, make every effort to respond to God's promises. Supplement your faith with a generous provision of moral excellence, and moral excellence with knowledge, and knowledge with self-control, and self-control with patient endurance, and patient endurance with godliness, and godliness with brotherly affection, and brotherly affection with love for everyone. The more you grow like this, the more productive and useful you will be in your knowledge of our Lord Jesus Christ. But those who fail to develop in this way are shortsighted or blind, forgetting that they have been cleansed from their old sins. So, dear brothers and sisters, work hard to prove that you really are among those God has called and chosen. Do these things and you will never fall away.

Prayer:

Thank You for developing and growing me. Father, You are helping me when I get weak or tired. Thank You, that You are more concerned about my growth than my comfort. Your tender love empowers me! Your spirit and Your word continually guide me through every trial! You are a good, good Father!

In Jesus' Name I pray

Amen

Scripture reference:

2 Peter 3:14

Therefore, beloved, as you anticipate these things, make every effort to be found at peace--spotless and blameless in His sight.

1 Samuel 2:26

And the boy Samuel continued to grow in stature and in favor with the LORD and with people.

Hebrews 6:1

Therefore, let us move beyond the elementary teachings about Christ and be taken forward to maturity, not laying again the foundation of repentance from acts that lead to death, and of faith in God

Jeremiah 12:2

2 You have planted them, and they have taken root; they grow and bear fruit. You are always on their lips but far from their hearts.

1 Peter 2:2, 3

Like newborn babies, crave pure spiritual milk, so that by it you may grow up in your salvation, now that you have tasted that the Lord is good.

Colossians 2:6, 7

So then, just as you received Christ Jesus as Lord, continue to live your lives in him, rooted and built up in him, strengthened in the faith as you were taught, and overflowing with thankfulness.

Hebrews 5:12-14

In fact, though by this time you ought to be teachers, you need someone to teach you the elementary truths of God's word all over again. You need milk, not solid food! Anyone who lives on milk, being still an infant, is not acquainted with the teaching about righteousness. But solid food is for the mature, who by constant use have trained themselves to distinguish good from evil.

Is God growing you in any of these areas in your life (physically, spiritually, emotionally etc.)? Ask the Lord to guide you in your answer:

------------------------------------------------------------------------

------------------------------------------------------------------------

------------------------------------------------------------------------

------------------------------------------------------------------------

------------------------------------------------------------------------

------------------------------------------------------------------------

------------------------------------------------------------------------

------------------------------------------------------------------------

------------------------------------------------------------------------

------------------------------------------------------------------------

------------------------------------------------------------------------

------------------------------------------------------------------------

------------------------------------------------------------------------

------------------------------------------------------------------------

------------------------------------------------------------------------

------------------------------------------------------------------------

------------------------------------------------------------------------

------------------------------------------------------------------------

------------------------------------------------------------------------

------------------------------------------------------------------------

------------------------------------------------------------------------

------------------------------------------------------------------------

# ALL THINGS ARE POSSIBLE

Devotional:

God brought forth our Savior from a virgin. He created a beautiful world from nothing by speaking it into existence. He raised dead people back to life. He turned water into wine. He healed the sick and performed many miracles.

Why do we doubt His ability to bring beauty from our ashes?

I was taking a walk with my friend one morning, when a bright yellow blooming flower, in the stony ground, caught our attention. It grew through the hard rocks and dusty ground, a good distance away from the beautiful green grass.

How many times do we find ourselves in lonely and dry places or even rocky, uncomfortable and painful situations? We may even see the Promised Land afar off, but don't know how to get there. We feel discouraged and tired, not realizing that God has purpose on our journey. Don't you know that He will allow you to produce and bloom even in the midst of these hard places?

As He brings you *out, forth, through and to* the Promised Land, you will BE the miracle that you prayed for. You will BE the answer to someone's prayer. Yield to the Lord in trust and complete surrender in every season. Not only will you find strength and peace, but others will be blessed by your life witness.


Scripture:

Luke 1:37

"For nothing will be impossible with God."

Prayer:

Thank You that You always have purpose in my life. Help me to see from Your perspective Father, knowing that You always work all things together for my good and Your glory. There is nothing impossible for You; and every step is divinely ordered by You. Let Your will be done, and Your kingdom come in my life.

In Jesus' Name I pray

Amen

Scripture Reference:

Genesis 18:14

Is anything too difficult for the LORD? At the appointed time I will return to you--in about a year--and Sarah will have a son."

Jeremiah 32:17

"Oh, Lord GOD! You have made the heavens and the earth by Your great power and outstretched arm. Nothing is too difficult for You!

Matthew 19:26

Jesus looked at them and said, "With man this is impossible, but with God all things are possible."

Luke 18:27

And he said, The things which are impossible with men are possible with God.

Numbers 11:23

And the LORD said unto Moses, Is the LORD'S hand waxed short? thou shalt see now whether my word shall come to pass unto thee or not.

Joshua 21:45 NIV

Not one of all the Lord's good promises to Israel failed; everyone was fulfilled.

Jeremiah 1:12 NIV

The Lord said to me, "You have seen correctly, for I am watching to see that my word is fulfilled."

What are the "impossible things" in your life which you feel you cannot achieve or overcome?

------------------------------------------------------------------------
------------------------------------------------------------------------
------------------------------------------------------------------------
------------------------------------------------------------------------
------------------------------------------------------------------------
------------------------------------------------------------------------
------------------------------------------------------------------------
------------------------------------------------------------------------
------------------------------------------------------------------------
------------------------------------------------------------------------
------------------------------------------------------------------------
------------------------------------------------------------------------
------------------------------------------------------------------------
------------------------------------------------------------------------
------------------------------------------------------------------------
------------------------------------------------------------------------
------------------------------------------------------------------------
------------------------------------------------------------------------
------------------------------------------------------------------------
------------------------------------------------------------------------
------------------------------------------------------------------------
------------------------------------------------------------------------
------------------------------------------------------------------------
------------------------------------------------------------------------

# SOVEREIGN GOD

Devotional:

Many years ago, my sister and I had a conversation about God. With the very limited knowledge we possessed, we attempted to figure out the "why's" and "how's" and in a very short time we realized we couldn't. My sister made a simple, but yet profound, statement that I will never forget. She exclaimed:" That's why God is God!!"

God reserves the secrets, the unknown, and the unexplainable in life for Himself; not to make us frustrated, but to trust Him fully. He sees the bigger picture. He sees every detail, every person, and every complexity. He knows the perfect timing and season for the manifestation of His promise and lets us know that we don't.

That's what makes Him God!  That's why He is sovereign!

God possesses supreme or ultimate power. His power is limitless. He is omniscient - all-knowing and all-seeing. God is in complete control, and *we are not*.

We find sweet rest and deep peace when we trust Him in the unknown.

Scripture:

Romans 11:33

"Oh, the depth of the riches of the wisdom and knowledge of God! How unsearchable his judgments, and his paths beyond tracing out!"

Prayer:

Father You are sovereign! I praise You with everything within me. I worship You just for who You are. You know every aspect of my life and You know the plans that You have for me. I am Your child and know that You are for me. When I have done all I know to do, I will trust You with the rest.

In Jesus' Name I pray

Amen

Scripture Reference:

Job 37:23

The Almighty is beyond our reach; He is exalted in power! In His justice and great righteousness He does not oppress.

Job 5:9

The One who does great and unsearchable things, wonders without number.

Psalm 135:6

Whatever the Lord pleases, He does, in heaven and in earth, in the seas and in all deeps.

Psalm 36:6

Your righteousness is like the highest mountains; Your judgments are like the deepest sea. O LORD, You preserve man and beast.

Psalm 92:5

How great are Your works, O LORD, how deep are Your thoughts!

Psalm 139:6

Such knowledge is too wonderful for me, too lofty for me to attain

Psalm 107:8

Oh that men would praise the LORD for his goodness, and for his wonderful works to the children of men!

Isaiah 46:10

Declaring the end from the beginning, and from ancient times things which have not been done, saying, 'My purpose will be established, and I will accomplish all my good pleasure'.

Ask the Lord if there is an area in your life where you still want to be in control?

--------------------------------------------------------------------------------
--------------------------------------------------------------------------------
--------------------------------------------------------------------------------
--------------------------------------------------------------------------------
--------------------------------------------------------------------------------
--------------------------------------------------------------------------------
--------------------------------------------------------------------------------
--------------------------------------------------------------------------------
--------------------------------------------------------------------------------
--------------------------------------------------------------------------------
--------------------------------------------------------------------------------
--------------------------------------------------------------------------------
--------------------------------------------------------------------------------
--------------------------------------------------------------------------------
--------------------------------------------------------------------------------
--------------------------------------------------------------------------------
--------------------------------------------------------------------------------
--------------------------------------------------------------------------------
--------------------------------------------------------------------------------
--------------------------------------------------------------------------------
--------------------------------------------------------------------------------
--------------------------------------------------------------------------------
--------------------------------------------------------------------------------

# My Strong Tower

Devotional:

It is vital to read the word of God daily. A beautiful transformation begins in us as we read, meditate and walk out the word of God. Our mind can easily be deceived, if we have not renewed it with the word of God. The word is like a fortress or stronghold that will protect us from false teachings, false prophets and or false prophecies. The word of God has the capability to discern lies from truth.

Hebrews 4:12 declares "For the word of God is quick, and powerful, and sharper than any two-edged sword, piercing even to the dividing asunder of soul and spirit, and of the joints and marrow, and is a discerner of the thoughts and intents of the heart".

In order to protect ourselves from the enemy we must have our fortress intact. If there are holes and openings, the enemy has free course to roam in our lives.

I had a couple of very busy days, and I kept pushing my time with the Lord back. I knew in my heart I needed to spend uninterrupted time with the Lord, to read His word and rest in His presence. During my busy time, I was listening to different messages from different pastors, in order to "get a word in". On the second day of doing that, I could sense confusion in my mind and did not feel my usual self. Everything seemed harder, and I did not sense the peace of God. It was not until I read my word and spent quality time with the Lord that His peace flooded my being again. The word of God is full of life.

Listening to all these different teaching brought confusion and disorder to my mind.

Am I saying we should not listen to other teachings? No, *but* we must keep our priorities right. God clearly tugged on my heart to spend time with HIM. He did not *lead me* to listen to another teaching. He wanted personal time with me. He wanted to pour into me.

We always have to keep our relationship with the Lord first!! The enemy is tricky and will use anything to keep us from the word of God and from talking to our Father. He will deceive us into thinking that listening to somebody's teaching is more than enough. He will deceive us into thinking that going to church is enough. As long as he can keep us out of the word of God, he's satisfied. He does not want us to receive the word of life. Satan knows, without our devotion to the Lord, our fortress will not be strong enough to keep him out.

The Lord is our stronghold and our firm foundation!!


Scripture:

Psalm 18:2

The LORD is my rock, my fortress and my deliverer; my God is my rock, in whom I take refuge, my shield and the horn of my salvation, my stronghold.

Prayer:

Lord thank You that your grace and mercy always draws me back to You. You are my rock, who gives me stability. Without You I can do nothing. Thank You for helping me and undergirding me, for nourishing and maturing me, to build your kingdom.

In Jesus' Name I pray

Amen

Scripture Reference:

1 Corinthians 3:11

For no man can lay a foundation other than the one which is laid, which is Jesus Christ.

Psalm 18:31

For who is God besides the LORD? And who is the Rock except our God?

Isaiah 28:16

Therefore thus says the Lord God, "Behold, I am laying in Zion a stone, a tested stone, a costly cornerstone for the foundation, firmly placed. He who believes in it will not be disturbed.

Psalm 144:2

My goodness, and my fortress; my high tower, and my deliverer; my shield, and he in whom I trust; who subdueth my people under me.

2 Samuel 22:3

The God of my rock; in him will I trust: he is my shield, and the horn of my salvation, my high tower, and my refuge, my saviour; thou savest me from violence.

Proverbs 18:10

The name of the LORD is a strong tower: the righteous runneth into it and is safe.

Psalm 9:9

The LORD is a refuge for the oppressed, a stronghold in times of trouble.

Ask the Father to reveal strongholds (wrong believe system) in your life.

Exchange those thoughts with God's word and speak His truth over your life:

Example: I renounce fear over my life. Father, You have not given me a spirit of fear, but of love and of a sound mind! There is no fear in love, but perfect love drives out fear. (2 Timothy 1:7; 1 John 4:18)

---

---

---

---

---

---

---

---

---

---

---

---

---

---

---

---

---

---

---

---

---

# Restoration

Devotional:

Webster defines restoration as: an act of restoring or the condition of being restored; a bringing back to a former position or condition.

God's will is to restore us, to heal us, and to bring us into our place of destiny-His heart!!

In Him we live, move and have our being. It is in Him where we truly REST. It is possible to walk in perfect peace, no matter what's going on around us. Jesus was able to sleep in the midst of a storm, because He had peace within Him and He was one with the Father (Mark 4:37-39).

Everything we do should flow from the heart of the Father down through our heart. He wants our heart close to His (Mark 7:6).

I experienced a lot growing up where God was not introduced to me in healthy and living way. It caused me to run from Him and build my life without Him. The enemy's goal is to keep us as far away from God as possible. Satan does not mind us having success and riches, as long as we don't make the Lord our foundation. Jesus is our cornerstone (see Ephesians 2:19-22)

My restoration process began when I responded to the call of God in my life. I had no godly foundation, so the Lord caused my foundation to collapse. Jesus Christ became my new foundation; and He started building my life in a brand-new exciting way. The process of restoring and rebuilding can be painful, but the result leads us to praise Him and recognize the beauty and wonders of His mighty hand over our lives.

Allow Jesus to be your foundation in family, business and all He leads you to build.

Scripture:

Joel 2:25, 26

"I will repay you for the years the locusts have eaten— the great locust and the young locust, the other locusts and the locust swarm — my great army that I sent among you. 26 You will have plenty to eat, until you are full, and you will praise the name of the LORD your God, who has worked wonders for you; never again will my people be shamed.

Prayer:

Father thank for Your faithfulness in my life. Restore me in Your love and mercy. I yield every part of me to You. Take over my life, my family, my job and everything in my life, because You can be trusted!

In Jesus' Name I pray

Amen

Scripture Reference:

Joel 2:25-26

I will restore to you the years that the swarming locust has eaten, the hopper, the destroyer, and the cutter, my great army, which I sent among you. "You shall eat in plenty and be satisfied, and praise the name of the Lord your God, who has dealt wondrously with you. And my people shall never again be put to shame.

1 Peter 5:10

And after you have suffered a little while, the God of all grace, who has called you to his eternal glory in Christ, will himself restore, confirm, strengthen, and establish you.

1 John 5:4

For everyone who has been born of God overcomes the world. And this is the victory that has overcome the world—our faith.

Zechariah 9:12

Return to your stronghold, O prisoners of hope; today I declare that I will restore to you double.

Psalm 23:1-6

A Psalm of David. The Lord is my shepherd; I shall not want. He makes me lie down in green pastures. He leads me beside still waters. He restores my soul. He leads me in paths of righteousness for his name's sake. Even though I walk through the valley of the shadow of death, I will fear no evil, for you are with me; your rod and your staff, they comfort me. You prepare a table before me in the presence of my enemies; you anoint my head with oil; my cup overflows.

Acts 3:21

Whom heaven must receive until the time for restoring all the things about which God spoke by the mouth of his holy prophets long ago.

Psalm 40:1-17

I waited patiently for the Lord; he inclined to me and heard my cry. He drew me up from the pit of destruction, out of the miry bog, and set my feet upon a rock, making my steps secure. He put a new song in my mouth, a song of praise to our God ....

Take a deep breath and allow the Lord to speak to your heart. Surrender any shortcomings:

---

# Resist the Enemy

Devotional:

Early this morning, my cat repeatedly tried to jump on my bed. He knows not to do that, but I had allowed him on the bed while my husband was out of town. I continued with my efforts to put him down, to no avail. At one point, I almost got tired of putting him down and let him rest for a minute, but then realized that it will be my consistency that will make him understand. Every time he jumped on the bed, I took him down and sprayed some water on him (cats dislike water), so that He understood our bed was no longer his resting place. Immediately I heard the Lord speak to me: "This is how the enemy will try you; resist him and be consistent."

We may have given the enemy permission or access to function in a specific area of our lives, but we can choose to close those doors. Anytime you take back what's yours, you will experience some level of warfare. The devil claims he has rights, but he doesn't. He will tempt us to the point of weariness so we will give in. He just needs one open door to continue his plan of destruction.

Stay alert and resist him. Remember that the devil disguises himself as an angel of light, but underneath his masquerade is a ravenous wolf. It is our job to consistently and boldly fight back and not allow weariness to compromise what we stand for.

Consistency combined with the water of the word causes the enemy to ultimately leave.

Scripture:

James 4:7 NIV

Submit yourselves, then, to God. Resist the devil, and he will flee from you.

Prayer:

Father, help me to continuously be sober-minded and alert, so I can recognize when the enemy seeks to devour me. Thank You for Your word that causes me to overcome every time. You are the One that trains my hands for war and my fingers for battle. I bless You Lord my strength!!!

In Jesus' Name I pray

Amen

Scripture Reference:

Ephesians 6:11

Put on the full armor of God, so that you can make your stand against the devil's schemes.

Ephesians 4:27

...and do not give the devil a foothold.

1 Peter 5:6-9

Humble yourselves, therefore, under God's mighty hand, so that in due time He may exalt you. Be sober-minded and alert. Your adversary the devil prowls around like a roaring lion, seeking someone to devour. Resist him, standing firm in your faith and in the knowledge that your brothers throughout the world are undergoing the same kinds of suffering

Matthew 4:3-11

And when the tempter came to him, he said, if thou be the Son of God, command that these stones be made bread. Jesus answered, "It is written: 'Man shall not live on bread alone, but on every word that comes from the mouth of God. Then the devil took him to the holy city and had him stand on the highest point of the temple. "If you are the Son of God," he said, "throw yourself down. For it is written: "'He will command his angels concerning you, and they will lift you up in their hands, so that you will not strike your foot against a stone. Jesus answered him, "It is also written: 'Do not put the Lord your God to the test.' Again, the devil took him to a very high mountain and showed him all the kingdoms of the world and their splendor. "All this I will give you," he said, "if you will bow down and worship me." Jesus said to him, "Away from me, Satan! For it is written: 'Worship the Lord your God and serve him only. Then the devil left him, and angels came and attended him.

Psalm 18:34-36

He teacheth my hands to war, so that a bow of steel is broken by mine arms. Thou hast also given me the shield of thy salvation: and thy right hand hath holden me up, and thy gentleness hath made me great. Thou hast enlarged my steps under me, that my feet did not slip.

Ask the Lord to show you any areas where you allowed the enemy access through negative words or actions. The same way you "announced" (declared) these things, now "renounce" (reject or surrender) them. Write these down and ask the Lord for divine strategies:

-------------------------------------------------------------------
-------------------------------------------------------------------
-------------------------------------------------------------------
-------------------------------------------------------------------
-------------------------------------------------------------------
-------------------------------------------------------------------
-------------------------------------------------------------------
-------------------------------------------------------------------
-------------------------------------------------------------------
-------------------------------------------------------------------
-------------------------------------------------------------------
-------------------------------------------------------------------
-------------------------------------------------------------------
-------------------------------------------------------------------
-------------------------------------------------------------------
-------------------------------------------------------------------
-------------------------------------------------------------------
-------------------------------------------------------------------
-------------------------------------------------------------------
-------------------------------------------------------------------
-------------------------------------------------------------------
-------------------------------------------------------------------

## About the Author

*Ursula McClary is a native of Heidelberg, Germany, currently residing in the Metro Atlanta area. She is passionate about making the love of Jesus Christ known through singing, teaching, praying, mentoring and by simply living and pursuing the life of Jesus Christ. She loves to serve and help people in need.*

*Currently she is a member at Word of Faith Family Worship Cathedral in Austell Georgia, where she serves in the Children Ministry and also facilitates a Life group for women.*

*Ursula is the author of "Journey to Freedom" and enjoys writing as the Lord leads. She is the Creator and founder of Ariel's Closet, where she uses her gifts and talents to handcraft art and accessories.*

*Ursula is also the founding leader of an online community called F.O.U.N.D. (Forgiven- Obedient - United - Noble- Daughters of God) to bring encouragement and help women in their Christian walk-through live videos, encouraging quotes, songs, and the word of God.*

*Her desire is to continue to share hope with everyone through her personal story and testimony of God's amazing redemptive power. She has been married to her husband, Van J. McClary, for 30 years. They have two beautiful grown daughters and two grandchildren.*

*Ursula's favorite scripture is found in Jeremiah 31:3 which states, "I have loved you with an everlasting love; I have drawn you with unfailing kindness."*

CPSIA information can be obtained
at www.ICGtesting.com
Printed in the USA
BVHW061017231222
654916BV00023B/964